Mister
Bones
Dinosaur Hunter

For David, my dinosaur-adoring boy —J. K.

For Pat, with love forever —M. H.

First Aladdin edition October 2004

Text copyright © 2004 by Jane Kurtz
Illustrations copyright © 2004 by Mary Haverfield

ALADDIN PAPERBACKS
An imprint of Simon & Schuster Children's Publishing Division
1230 Avenue of the Americas
New York, NY 10020

All rights reserved, including the right of
reproduction in whole or in part in any form.

READY-TO-READ is a registered trademark of Simon & Schuster.

Book design by Lisa Vega
The text of this book was set in CenturyOldst BT.

Printed in the United States of America
2 4 6 8 10 9 7 5 3 1

Library of Congress Cataloging-in-Publication Data

Kurtz, Jane.
Mister Bones: dinosaur hunter / by Jane Kurtz ; illustrated by Mary
Haverfield.
p. cm. — (Ready-to-read)
ISBN 978-0-689-85960-1
1. Brown, Barnum—Juvenile literature. 2. Paleontologists—United
States—Biography—Juvenile literature. [1. Brown, Barnum.
2. Paleontologists. 3. Scientists. 4. Tyrannosaurus rex. 5. Dinosaurs.
6. Fossils.] I. Title: Mister Bones. II. Haverfield, Mary, ill. III. Title.
IV. Series.
QE707.B77K87 2004
560'.92—dc22

2003024534

Mister Bones
Dinosaur Hunter

By Jane Kurtz
Illustrated by Mary Haverfield

Aladdin
New York   London   Toronto   Sydney

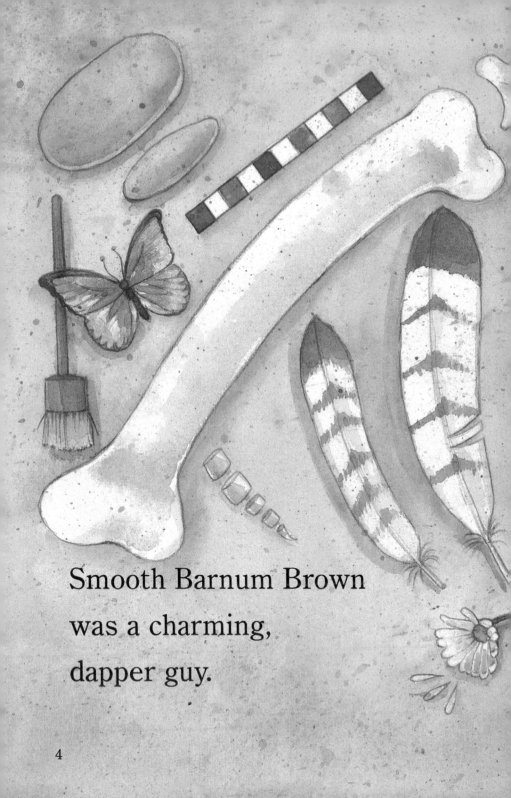

Smooth Barnum Brown
was a charming,
dapper guy.

He went climbing over rocks
in a topcoat and a tie.

He loved ballroom dancing,
but he was not dancing now.
He was digging in the dirt.
What was he looking for?

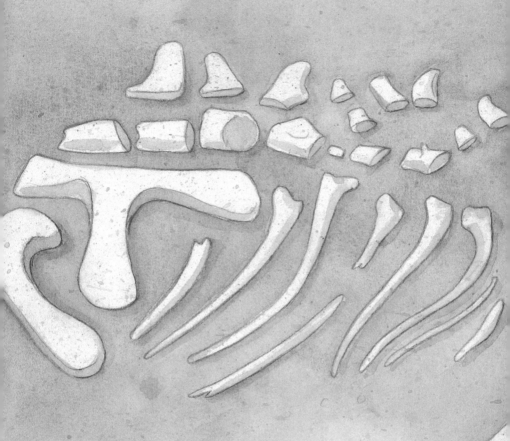

It was not shining silver.
His wife once
called it rainbows,
but it was not in the sky.

Others wore bandannas
and cowboy boots and chaps.
Mister Brown came to Montana
in a fancy coat and hat.

He poked and he sifted
and he picked in the dirt.
Was he hunting gold?
No, nothing quite that old.

But what he hunted
people wanted
just about as much as gold.
Bones. Big old bones.

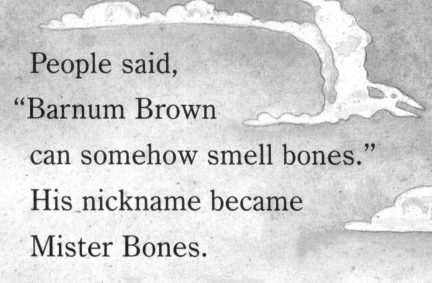

People said,
"Barnum Brown
can somehow smell bones."
His nickname became
Mister Bones.

Mister Bones found bones
in the middle of Montana—
a backbone and a hip bone
and other bones and chips.

Bones were packed in boxes,
shipped off to New York.
Putting them together
took lots and lots of work.

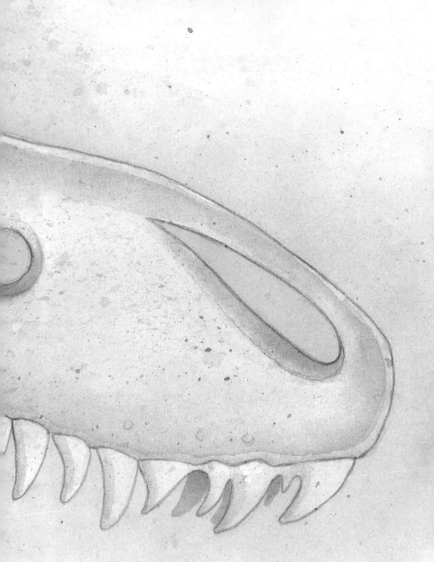

Step back! Imagine that!
Now what about a name?
A name? Yes, a name
for this amazing thing.

That job went
to the museum president.

Henry Osborn called it
tyrant lizard king.

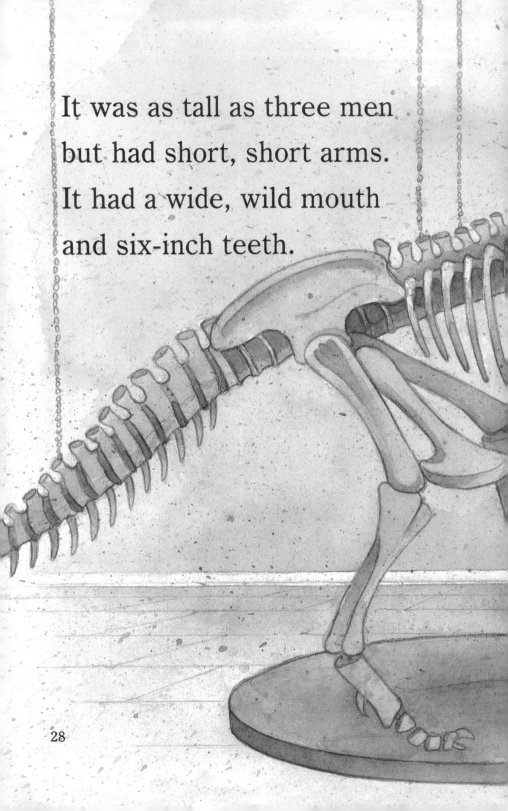

It was as tall as three men
but had short, short arms.
It had a wide, wild mouth
and six-inch teeth.

Huge Tyrannosaurus.

Gigantic T. Rex.

Mister Bones had found
the tyrant lizard king.